Intakes: it's been (Xenorama was publisheu ... ... and paper form. It's kind of a cliché to say "the world has changed a lot" in that time frame, but it's true. As of this writing (August 2010) I am not even sure what will be in this new issue, but at least there will be a new one.

The best thing out there now is Publish On Demand. I upload the contents of the book (or magazine) to an online publisher, and then direct all of the people that want to buy the book to them. Then I don't have to shell out all that money, except to get contributors their copies.

Chances are it'll be a one or two man show this time around!

There are a lot of reasons for the long absence of the fanzine, none of which are really germane to any kind of discussion here. Suffice it to say, Xenorama is back!

This issue is dedicated to the late Peter Fernandez.

All content © their respective creators and/or owners (i.e. Toho, Marvel, etc). Thanks to my co-editor Chris Elam, and my valued contributors Dan Ross, Tara DeVeau, Chad McAlpin, Mike Lawyer and Jeff Goodhartz. Unless credited, everything in here is written by me.

Xenorama, A History

"Everyone is entitled to my opinion." ~Anonymous

Sometime in late 1991 or early 1992 I was inspired to publish my own fanzine. This came about from reading Damon Foster's groundbreaking *Oriental Cinema* and *Monster! International*, among several other magazines being published at the time. I was writing a small article on **The Magic Serpent** (1966) for Oriental Cinema and somehow it turned into the centerpiece for the first issue of Xenorama.

The name of my zine was a bit of a challenge. After discussions with a few friends I settled on "Xenorama" and have been using it ever since then. I didn't realize that I had actually coined a word.

I had no idea what I was doing in those early days. I put out a call for contributions and received several. I typed up my pieces, then went to a local copy shop and shrunk them down, cut and pasted (quite literally) the whole thing together and voila! Instant fanzine. I wish I had been able to get better reproductions of the images I used, as that was always something that I didn't like. I didn't have a nifty computer at the time, and only a few people had these scanner things that one could add pictures right into the computer.

After publishing three issues in a year, I was getting the hang of it. I could borrow computers from friends and at least be able to correct typos if I noticed them. Of course, I usually only noticed them well after publication, which was not that much fun. I am sure this will happen again in this issue, but that's how publication goes.

Then real life struck
and it publishing the
issues slowed down to two,
or maybe just one issue a
year. It wasn't until about
issue #6 (the underwater
issue) that I really felt like
Xenorama had found it's
unique voice. Sure, there
were still some poorly written
contributions on my part, but
overall I really like the rest of
the issues and am more
impressed with them when I
read them now.

Summertime, 96   volume 1 issue 9

$2.00

XENORAMA

the Journal of Heroes and Monsters

Robots!

issue #9

One of the things I
promised myself was
that Godzilla would always
have a presence in
the magazine. This was
before I had discovered G-Fan (they started publishing around
the same time, I think) and I always thought there was never
enough Godzilla in any genre magazine. Naturally I was right
about that! So while there was no article on Godzilla in issue #1,
there he was on the cover. After that, there was always an
article about Godzilla featured in every issue, and plenty of
pictures (such as I could find, pre-internet).

The zine fluctuated between two sizes, depending on
what sort of processes I had access to- it was about evenly split
between the large standard paper size and the digest size, which
I preferred. The digest size was always cheaper in the long run!
I and my many contributors soldered on, producing 14 complete
issues in less than 10 years. Not bad for someone who was
completely self taught about magazine publishing.

During this time I got mentioned by several other
fanzines, and real magazines as well. Those plugs were always
very kind. I'd like to thank *G-Fan, Cult Movies, Kaiju Review,
Owari, Psychotronic, Giant Robot, Yum* and many others that
have now long escaped my brain banks.

One of the other things that Xenorama inadvertantly inspired me to do was write for other magazines. Including several of the ones I mentioned above, I wrote articles for *Oriental Cinema* (Damon finally got a review of **THE MAGIC SERPENT**) and *The Prehistoric Times*.

During it's run, I added several various columns to cover things not related to the issues main theme, such as "Thunderfoot Theater", "The Serial Box", "Xenosonica"... now it looks like I sort of cluttered the magazine with too much stuff. I can see now I wanted to write about other stuff as well, such as music and pro-wrestling, but again, I think it was too much for the zine.

As time marched on, and the Internets became more and more accessible, the whole fanzine fad kind of faded out, with more and more zines ending their runs. I had intended to continue publishing, and actually had about half of the original issue #15 done when real life again intruded (darn it) and the zine itself was put on hold. Somewhere I have those pages for the previous issue fifteen, maybe they will see the light of day sometime in the future.

The original zine was never very financially successful, except for the final issue. I actually made money on that one. That also led to lapse of several years, as I couldn't afford to keep publishing a magazine I wasn't breaking even on. I didn't want to make millions of dollars, but not losing any money would be good too.

So now it's 2013 and what has changed? Inspiration struck with the fine magazine Monster Attack Team having a new issue published in 2010, and also with the arise of "print on demand" sites. That makes publishing a lot more cost effective. So enjoy the new Xenorama!

CHRISTOPHER ELAM'S OWARI

(OWARI #13)

BEEN THIS WAY, TEN YEARS TO THE DAY

Golly, has it really been almost a decade since the last issue of **XENORAMA**? During that time, I published two more issues of **OWARI**, but decided it was time to end my own fanzine with #12. But that's OK, because I've kept the fire burning even without a print forum. I'll tell you where else you can find me at the end of this column.

I submitted an installment of "The Ranger Report" to David many years ago for this issue, and he *may* even find a spot for it here. However, I think it's time to retire that old column name for any new works of mine in **XENORAMA**. I mean, after all, there is a perfectly good name that's not being used for a fanzine anymore. So say hello to the first installment (of many?) of "Christopher Elam's OWARI" in **XENORAMA**!

BEHOLD, THE MIRACLE OF TWIN EARTHS!

I really don't get that excited about most comic books anymore. There are a lot of reasons for that, and I don't have an entire book to outline them for you. Suffice to say, it takes something pretty special to get me jazzed about driving to the comics store. Usually, it involves stuff that I recall fondly from my hilariously misspent youth.

The **CRISIS ON MULTIPLE EARTHS** books more than fit that bill for me. **CRISIS ON MULTIPLE EARTHS** is a series of trade paperbacks that reprints the classic annual team-ups of the Justice League of America and Justice Society of America in chronological order starting from the beginning in 1963. This is back in the days when "cosmic" stories and superhero team-ups didn't happen every single week, so these stories held a special cachet that your average super duper epic lacks today.

I loved the JLA/JSA team-ups when I was a kid. It fascinated me that there was a parallel Earth (Earth-2) with alternate versions of familiar heroes like Flash and Green Lantern, teaming with unique and different characters like the Sandman and Dr. Fate. I had no idea originally of the unique history that led to the JLA/JSA dichotomy, but I was eager to learn, and it made me love the stories all the more.

Depicted here is the cover to the first volume of the series, with an eye-catching Alex Ross cover. These are the stories that reunite the JSA as a fighting force and reintroduce many of the classic characters of DC's Golden Age. Further installments upped the stakes by bringing in other teams, including the Seven Soldier of Victory (my favorite JLA/JSA story, from *Justice League of America* #100-#102) and the Legion of Super-Heroes (my first, from 1977, in #147-#148).

Gardner Fox, the man who created both the Justice League *and* the Justice Society, is the writer who scripted the bulk of the stories in these volumes. Later tales come from the likes of Denny O'Neil, Mike Friedrich, Len Wein, and Gerry Conway. The penciling is supplied by Mike Sekowsky and Dick Dillin, two seriously underrated artists who performed yeoman-like duties in bringing dozens of characters to life.

There have been five volumes in this series, with the fifth having only recently arrived in stores in 2010. There is also a spin-off series entitled *CRISIS ON MULTIPLE EARTHS : THE TEAM-UPS*, which has reprinted other E-1/E-2 team-ups in two volumes. There could conceivably be two additional volumes in the main *CRISIS* line, and possibly even further editions in its companion series. Boy, I sure hope so!

If you'd like a dose of cosmic superhero action back in the days when that didn't mean a huge investment in time and brainpower, check out these books. They are among my favorites on my own bookshelf.

SENTAI HERO SHUGO!

I've spent a lot of time in this 'zine discussing the Japanese superhero sentai genre, so it seems only appropriate to give it a mention in this grand comeback. And what better choice could I make than to review the amazing *GAORANGER VS. SUPER SENTAI*?

Toei Video has been releasing these "VS" team-up movies since the mid-1990s, but in 2001 (has it really been that long?), they tried a different tack. Instead of Gaoranger, the then-current sentai, joining forces with their predecessors from the previous year, they found themselves allied with a sentai all-star team with members dating back to the 1970s!

This sentai movie is unique in that it really is a feature-length film. This is accomplished by crafty means indeed – not only is there a main plot, but there are also plenty of excuses for flashbacks, too. Yes, this is that old staple of Japanese superheroes, the highlight reel/clipshow. It's good stuff too, and it really emphasizes all the good qualities of the sentai genre through the years. OK, yes, maybe the bad, too, but that is part of the charm!

The acting and FX are about what you should expect from sentai – uneven, but endearingly so. I have got to think that is part of the quirky appeal for a lot of fans. While these shows are filled with stirring action and intriguing stories, sometimes it just feels good to see a stuntman dubbed by a newbie actor whaling the blue blazes out of another stuntman dressed as a sewing machine monster. Those are good times, and *GAORANGER VS. SUPER SENTAI* has that in abundance.

GAORANGER VS. SUPER SENTAI also has Hiroshi Miyauchi reprising his role as Shokichi Banba, aka "Big One" from the show *JAKQ*. I have made no secret of the fact that

Miyauchi is my favorite superhero actor of all time, and I don't just mean Japanese superheroes either. He pretty easily steals the movie, and even teams with himself in one of the about six or seven "Wow!" moments in this video.

GAORANGER VS. SUPER SENTAI is a great way to introduce yourself or someone you know to the sentai genre. You may not like it, but you'll sure know what everyone is talking about after you've watched it!

DON'T TASE ME, BRO! And now, a few words about the

most exciting music news of the year 2010 as far as I was concerned: namely, Devo released their first new studio album since 1990! *Something For Everybody* is an exciting and dynamic return to form for the spudboys that somehow manages to be the best Devo album since at least 1982. Believe me, I was prepared to be disappointed by this release, and it won me over. The most promising thing about this album is that it is both musically and lyrically satisfying. In songs like "Fresh", "What We Do", "Please Baby Please" and "Don't Shoot (I'm A Man)", Devo manages to recapture the energy and bite that made them idiosyncratic cult favorites who stood out even in the punk and new wave movements. *Something For Everybody* is not Devo 2.0, nor is it old songs repackaged for commercial jingles. It is Devo the way they were in their prime, and even if it's just another pose, it's still good to have a reminder of what that used to mean. Seek out this release, either on CD, vinyl, or download, and see if you agree that it's the Devo album you've been waiting for all these years!

(Christopher Elam is a freelance writer and raconteur living in what he likes to refer to as "the boot-shaped state". He has written for G-FAN, KAIJU REVIEW, ORIENTAL CINEMA, and of course, XENORAMA. You can currently find him writing about whatever strikes his fancy at http://christopherelam.blogspot.com. You can follow him on this Twitter thing at http://twitter.com/celamowari. He really likes the word "raconteur".)

INFRAMAN

The ad copy for this film reads "The Man Beyond Bionics"; an allusion to the then popular stateside shows of the day. However, it is so far above the rather anemic *Six Million Dollar Man* and *Bionic Woman* that the comparison is laughable. It also says the movie is the "Ultimate in Science Fiction" and while *that* statement may be hyperbole, as I have titled this article, it *is* the ultimate in super hero movies.

A little background first. I had heard of this film in a magazine called "*King Of the Monsters*" (oddly enough, not referring to Godzilla). This was a one shot mainly devoted to the remake of **King Kong**, naturally trying to capitalize on the hype surrounding the film. It's always the way, though. Back before the internet, when a film came along that was *supposed* to capture the public (both their dollars and imagination), there were always several hundred various items rising up to make sure they get a piece of the pie. But I'm always glad, as the exploitative stuff usually was more fun and had more hidden gems in it than what it was trying to make money on.

Now what prompted me to purchase this piece of exploitative journalism? Well, mostly for Don Glut's excellent article "Godzilla, Superhero of the Seventies". It was ostensibly about **GODZILLA VS. MEGALON**, it mainly dealt with the state of screen heroes at that time. It also had some great photos that I had never seen before. None of which were from the movie, but that was OK with me. I just wanted to see Godzilla pictures.

(As a side note, this was also the first time I had really read a genuine, well done, positive and respectful article about Godzilla- I thanked him in person back at G-Fest 99.)

Aside from that article, and the ones on the piece of crap *King Kong* remake, there were nice pieces on **ONE MILLION YEARS BC**, various gorillas in films, **THE CRATER LAKE MONSTER**, and **INFRA-MAN VS. THE VOLCANO MONSTERS**, AKA **INFRA-MAN** (by Stan Karpels).

Made by the always astounding Shaw Brothers during their 70s heyday, this was what some might call a "rip-off" (I prefer homage) of various Japanese heroes such as Kikaida, Kamen Rider and Ultraman (especially the last two), all vastly popular in Asia at the time, and still are, incidentally. These are what are known as *"henshin"* or transforming heroes, due to their propensity to change from one form to another.

The plot was covered- blond Princess Dragon-Mom (the lovely Terry Liu Hui-ju) returns to life, and along with her army of monsters and robots, is ready to take over the world!

Fortunately for the Earth and us humans, Professor Chang (Wang Hsieh) has developed plans for the super-human Inframan. All he needs is a volunteer brave enough to "endure the fires of hell" and be transformed. Luckily Lt. Rayma (Li Hsiu Hsien) is ready and able to undergo the dangerous procedure. The good doctor is successful and Inframan takes on the Princess's monsters one by one, until we are taken to the princess' base where there is a final battle royal-fight to the finish between Inframan, Princess Dragon-Mom and her remaining monsters.

All this in four pages!! Add to that some great pictures, and my imagination was fired, I'll tell you what!

As fate would have it, I lived in a small town at the time. And the Theater Gods decreed **INFRAMAN** would not grace the silver screen in Longmont, Colorado (this happened a lot- those darn gods!). To top matters off, a year or two later I met a fellow (he knows who he is) who *had* seen the film, and he claimed that the critters looked like the horrible *"Sigmund and the Sea Monsters"*! Yuck! What could be worse? Of course, when I saw the famous **Sneak Previews** "Guilty Pleasures" show in the early 80s, I could see how wrong he was, but that was my only exposure to the film for almost ten years.

Now we flash forward from the early 80s to the mid-80s. VCRs are becoming common, mom-and-pop video stores are sprouting up like weeds (we are also paying $10 to $25 "membership" fees) and we can actually rent movies instead of waiting for them to air on TV at some ungodly hour. So one fateful trip, while browsing through the rather anemic "Sci-fi" section, there on the shelf staring back at me was the heroic visage of Inframan! Grasping the box in my hot little hands, I informed my friends (in a tone that brooked no argument) that "We <u>are</u> renting this movie!" and away we went.

As I had mentioned earlier, I had seen a few clips from *Sneak Previews*. I thought I had a vague inkling of what to expect. I had also seen a few episodes of *Ultraman*, and thought this would look a little something like that. There was no way I could have been properly prepared for what I would be witnessing.

I could hardly believe what I was seeing- monsters, robots, heroes, villainesses (rather sexy ones at that) laser rays and martial arts. I wasn't prepared for the images that were presented to my eyes. I couldn't have been, there was no way to be adequately prepared. It took at least three or four years for it all to settle into my brain properly, and several more viewings.

This is a movie that offers no apology for it's concept. Too many American superhero shows and movies often seem ashamed to show their hero in full regalia, or give them flashy villains to fight. But not in Asia! They are proud of what they are doing, and know that their audience wants to see a super hero in action. And they give the audience what they want- in spades! It also helps that the actors can actually fight, and the director doesn't have to resort to quick choppy edits to make it appear the stars are fighting.

The flick zooms by at top speed, and only slows down once for a bit of character development between the Prof. and his daughter Mei-Mei (Yuan Man-chi). But as soon as the father-daughter moment is over, it's back to fights and monsters. We also have a few goofy kid antics, but considering the main audience of the film, that's OK as well. In this ninety-minute film you get about ten minutes to rest. Pretty good timing, I think. During the massive amounts of fights, Inframan takes on a variety of monsters- some plantlike, some robot, and in an incredible mid-movie fight, enlarges to take on a raspy voiced spider monster. This provides one of the movies most memorable moments: after defeating the spider-thingie, it shrinks back to normal size and Infra-man, still giant, walks over and **ker-spalt!** - stomps on it, shooting out gross green blood from under his foot. Though, what else would you do to a spider-monster, right? This is accompanied by the appropriate squishy sound effects. What makes this unusual is the fact that most Japanese monsters usually explode upon defeat. I guess prehistoric Hong Kong monsters have a different chemical make up.

There are of course, the obligatory "throw-around" hench-robots (I call 'em Skull-bots [copyright 2013 David McRobie]) that are equal to ordinary fighters, but explode when hit with one of our hero's mighty punches.

Nearly all the monsters have a variety of rays, laser beams and weapons that they can use against Infra-man, who has all of the above and more to fight back with as well. I'm not sure who supervised the special effects, but they are wonderful. I believe it could have been a Japanese technician brought over by the Shaw Studio, as they did with Sademasa Arikawa for 1977's **MIGHTY PEKING MAN** (AKA **GOLIATHON** re-released by good ol' Quentin Tarantino- available on R1 DVD and Blu-Ray) also starring Li Hsiu Hsien. But this is all conjecture on my part. The monster making company, X Productions of Japan, was uncredited in the film as well. Can you guess what they contributed to the movie? When Inframan grows to giant size to take on the red spider monster, it's a nice little tip of the hat to Ultraman.

The only monster that doesn't fire a laser beam of some kind, is a grumbling, surly, green hulk called Nemesis in the US dub. This critter has a great personality, and has to do a lot of the Princess' dirty work, such as capturing Tu Ming (Lin Wen-wei) and planting a bomb in the science headquarters. Good thing Infra-man is around to stop him. He's tough enough to take on Inframan bare handed, er, clawed! And all the monsters, henchmen and good guys know kung fu of some kind. It's amazing that martial arts are so widespread all over Asia- even 10,000 years before they were invented!

The fighting style Inframan uses is also very unique. The Shaw Brothers studio style was Hung Gar, a southern style of kung fu. But the ancient forms and weapons don't really cut it fighting prehistoric monster-men. So we have an unusual amalgam of Japanese monster fighting and Chinese kung fu. It works really well, and is very theatrical. The fighting instructor was Tang Chia, who admirably creates a very unusual, visual style. I wonder how many people got hurt from the explosions that occur- those costumes are not easy to fight in and have very limited vision. A lot of time and practice was needed before they could roll film.

The rest of the cast is as fine as one can tell, being dubbed. There are no real name stars of the Shaws', like Fu Sheng, Lo Mang or Chen Kwan Tai. Li Hsiu Hsien also starred in the "bio-pic" **BRUCE LEE, HIS LAST DAYS, HIS LAST NIGHTS**, but that isn't really worth mentioning here. He's still actively working, both acting and directing, as Danny Lee these days and has been in some John Woo movies.

One interesting side note: the character of Hsu Long (a sergeant) is played by Huan Chien-lung, who later became known as Bruce Le. Most of his cheap movies are available for your viewing pleasure at local stores. Look 'em up yourself if you want to know the titles. You can tell he is being groomed for starring roles, as he gets a fair share of camera time during the action scenes. Peter Fernandez, whom I will discuss in a little bit, also dubbed him.

Of course, one of the main reasons to watch this film is, of course, the lovely Princess Dragon-mom. As neat looking as she is, she sure is evil. In fact, she is pure evil. She can fight pretty well, but she just lives to conquer the world. Unlike other female villains, such as Catwoman, Su Muru or even Lois Lane, there is no goodness or humanity in her heart, if she has one, at all. After all, she is a really some sort of ancient dragon creature. So the visual appeal is there, but there is no emotional subtext to her. Not that she deserves one. But her unrepentant villainy makes her fun to watch. You can at least admire the conviction of her beliefs. And of course, you can cheer when Inframan absolutely kicks her butt.

Skeleton Warriors and Ice Monsters, come out!

Peter Fernandez, who many of us listened to in many Japanese movies, and was also the voice of Speed Racer, wrote the English dialogue (he also wrote the English dialog for many of the movies and TV shows he worked on, notably *MOTHRA* (1961), **Ultraman** and the Godzilla and Gamera movies, among many, many others). His long time partner in dubbing, Corrine Orr is also in the voice cast. She did the voices of Mei Mei and the little kids. The dubbing is handled very well, and there are no voices saying "But still..." or "I reckon..." in this film. The lips sinc up as much as possible, and sound fairly natural as well. It's always pleasant to hear familiar voices in a movie like this.

Recently the Hong Kong based DVD company Celestial has been releasing the over 700 movie Shaw Brothers Catalog onto Region 3 DVD. These have been nothing less than nearly flawless transfers- picture and sound looks great. The subs sometimes leave a bit to be desired, and also missing are the classic English dubbed tracks, but for the most part the quality of the films themselves is superb. There are people out there who can tell you if some music has been replaced, or if a movie is cut but I am not one of them.

Naturally, one of the films they have released is **THE SUPER INFRAMAN**! It's very interesting to watch the Chinese version of the movie, and hear the Mandarin or Cantonese language. It's a tad more serious than the US version. I'm so used to hearing the dubbed voices it seems like the movie has been re-dubbed to me! The subtitled dialogue matches up pretty well with the dubbing, although some changes have been made to sound better to English audiences. Some slight humor was added, which seems to be a trademark of Peter Fernandez' writing style (see both "*Marine Boy*" and "*Speed Racer*" for some prime examples of this humor). He is also responsible for many of the trademark lines of dialogue, which are nowhere near as funny in the subtitled version. However, the name "Princess Elzibub" just doesn't stack up with "Princess Dragon-mom" now, does it?

The Region 3 DVD looks wonderful. The director, Hua Shan really makes use of the widescreen photography. The action goes back and forth across the screen all the time. It makes the legit VHS English panned and scanned tape look all the worse. The sound is excellent as well. You have the choice of either Mandarin or Cantonese language tracks to listen to as well. It also sounds great. Some of the sound effects are different from the US version as well, and the US opening is actually better than the original, if not as complete. Much of the original music was also eliminated or changed. Again, the US version is an improvement here. The unique sound effects are all the same, but I'm thinking that the entire soundtrack was redone completely. This is unusual, since most Asian films came with two audio tracks back then, the dialogue and then everything else. It could have been re-done like this to make the "stereo-infra sound" claim legitimate, although who would possibly know what that is supposed to sound like?

An interesting note for those "sub-elitists"- the people who won't watch any movie unless it's in the original language- all Chinese films were shot silently until the mid-90s, and then later had the voices dubbed in. A lot of times it was not done by the original actor, so in essence, all these movies are dubbed anyway, either in English or Mandarin or Cantonese or other languages. Many actors in Hong Kong did not speak both dialects of Chinese. This is also why they were subtitled in Chinese, as everyone reads the same kanji. They were subtitled in English because the British wanted to know what the characters were saying, and possibly to make sure they weren't passing some kind of anti-British statements along with the movies. At least that's one theory I've read somewhere.

Now we have Damon Foster's excellent comprehensive issue of Oriental Cinema (issue #23) on this fine film. If you want to know even more about this movie, seek out this fine publication. Of course, Damon has his own writing style, so keep that in mind. You can order it here-http://www.lilsproutz.com/DF/products.htm.

In October of 2006 Image Entertainment released **THE CHINESE SUPERMAN** on DVD here in the Western Hemisphere. The picture is nearly identical to the R3 disc. It contains the Mandarin dub with fine, readable English subtitles. It also includes the excellent dub, though apparently it was taken from a video tape source, so there is one instance of the sound dropping (about 18 minutes into the movie). It is noticeably quieter than the Chinese track, but it's not enough to complain about, though plenty of online spoiled fanboys already have. Apparently they can't remember a time (about 5 years ago) where a DVD of this type would have been unheard of, much less a possibility to get released. We are missing both the US opening and any promotional materials to the movie as well, which can also be attributed to Brenner's lack of participation.

There is also a fine booklet included, with liner notes written by Damon Foster and August Ragone. It might actually contain more information in it than Oriental Cinema does, but you will have to decide for yourself.

I'm not quite sure why this would be on anyone's list of "guilty pleasures". It's not a pretentious movie at all, nor is it awful. It doesn't show women or children getting brutalized, there is no swearing or nudity in it- of course, that may be a detriment to some viewers, but it makes the movie great for families with kids, and we need more movies like that, in these days of "dark, gritty and realistic" heroes who are hard to differentiate from the villains on occasion.

Inframan and the Professor confer on tactics

This is, to this day, the most action packed superhero/sci-fi/monster/adventure movie ever made. All that's missing to make it the greatest film ever is Godzilla, but that might be just a little too much goodness in one movie. It certainly shouldn't be *anyone's* guilty pleasure. As for my friend who described them as the atrocious *Sigmund* show, I haven't let him live that down yet. To try to describe it in any more detail is to negate the impact of the film itself. It was one of the last imports from Asia to receive a theatrical releasing. In the years that followed, cartoons became much more "the thing" to watch. Well, give me three-dimensional action over cartoons any day. Exciting, fun, thrilling, all are correct adjectives to describe... the Man Beyond Bionics... **Inframan!**

(most of this article appeared in G-Fan several years ago, as part of my "Globe Meter" series. It has been updated a bit for this publication. I'm also slightly annoyed that I've thought the name of this movie was "Infra-man" for years, never noticing there was no hyphen in the movie's title...)

Godzilla's Revenge (1969)

an appreciation

by Mike Lawyer

The 1969 Toho Company, Limited film Godzilla's Revenge is one of the most maligned and misunderstood monster films ever made. Originally released in Japan as Oru Kaiju Daishingeki (All Monsters Attack) this was the tenth film in the Godzilla series. Made for a fraction of the budget of the previous films, most of the monster action was culled from stock footage from earlier Godzilla films, and the plot was a bizarre departure from the standard giant monster movie that left most fans scratching their heads and ultimately disliking the film intensely. However if examined more closely, the film is actually a statement on modern Japan and the neglect of children in an increasingly industrialized society. The plot features a young boy, Ichiro, who is a fairly average kid-he is bullied by older kids at school, his parents both work and he is left alone at their apartment everyday after school with sporadic supervision by a kindly older neighbor named Minami. To escape the drudgery and loneliness of his everyday life, Ichiro has vivid daydreams of visiting Monster Island and befriending Godzilla's son Minya. In his daydreams Minya, who is usually 18 meters tall, can shrink down to boy size and can also speak. The two friends watch Godzilla battle other titanic denizens of the island (the stock footage from previous movies) and deal with a huge bullying monster named Gabara that constantly picks on Minya. Finally Godzilla teaches Minya to stand up for himself and the baby monster defeats the larger bully beast, after which Gabara stupidly picks a fight with Godzilla himself and is soundly trounced. Using the lessons learned from Godzilla and Minya, Ichiro is able to outwit two inept bank robbers that kidnap him and also to stand up to the bullying kids, who then become his friends. However, Ichiro's sad home life has not changed and his falling in with the gang of bully kids is not exactly a happy ending.

The film was meant by director Ishiro Honda to be an examination and condemnation of the neglect of children. Unlike all the other Godzilla films that take place in an alternate reality where science is advanced with laser weapons and spaceships, Godzilla's Revenge takes place squarely in the real world in a dirty, industrial section of Tokyo with drab apartment conplexes, ruined abandoned buildings and unsupervised children. Ichiro is alone and unsupervised for 90% of the film. At the end of the movie, after Ichiro has used the lessons he learned from Godzilla and Minya to outwit the bank robbers, Minami says to the boy." Let's take you home." To which Ichiro replies tearfully," But no one is there." To me that scene sums up the entire point of the film. The final shot of the movie is on the surface a happy scene of Ichiro running off with his new friends, the gang of neighborhood bullies, but how happy an ending is this really? Nothing in Ichiro's home life has changed, he is still a latch key kid, and he still is loose to play in the dirty industrial area and in the dangerous ruined buildings, plus he is now part of the bully gang. I believe director Honda, who usually tried to incorporate a relevant social commentary into most of his monster and sci-fi movies, meant this to show that Japan's industrial and economic resurgence that bloomed throughout the '60's was not necessarily a good thing for Japan's children.

Released by **U Q A UNITED PRODUCTIONS OF AMERICA**   **GODZILLA'S REVENGE**   Distributed by MARON FILMS LIMITED
COLOR

I feel that this movie's message is probably even more relevant today than it was forty years ago, and not just in Japan. Latch key children became an issue in the '80's in the United States as more and more families had to have both parents work, and today I believe it is more rampant than ever. Today a stay at home parent is very much the exception rather the rule. Fortunately my sister and myself were never latch key children and my wife and I have always been able to have one of us home to watch our two sons, but I knew many children that were latch key kids from my generation and my boys know a lot of them as well, and these kids seem to be much more likely to get into trouble by either doing or being someplace they shouldn't because there is no parental supervision or to trying drugs and alcohol at a young age.

original ad matte for Godzilla's Revenge

Moby Dick Episode Guide

Two young boys, Tom and Tub, are swept overboard and surrounded by sharks. The great white whale Moby Dick saves them. They happily realize they have a new friend who helps protect them from a variety of dangerous sea life, villains and invaders.

With that, Hanna-Barbera unleashed it's most ungainly series in the fall of 1967. Just where Tom and Tubb are is never explained, nor how they got Scooby the sea lion, nor if they have parents looking for them, and the kids never even try to return home. Other odd things are what do they eat, how do they replenish their air supply, things like that. I mean, I know not to try to apply too much logic to a 6 minute cartoon series, but perhaps the premise could have been fleshed out a bit more.

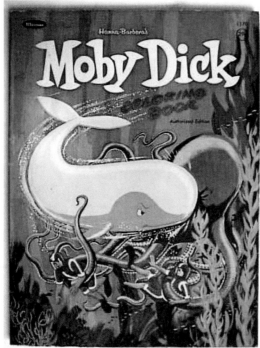

coloring book

Having said that, the cartoon is a lot of fun. The kids are never annoying, it's an interesting hero, the villains and monsters are all well designed and the undersea setting is unique. One can see the genius that was Alex Toth easily here. The episodes are action packed, but of course, at 6 minutes, they can't really help that!

There were a few tie ins with comic books and coloring books with the Hanna-Barbera heroes. Gold-Key released seven issues of "Super TV Heroes" and each had a Moby Dick story in it. These were done in 1968. There are no credits to the artwork, but it's not bad at all. I had the coloring book, and so far, it's been the only one I could find from the Hanna-Barbera heroes that I could find (I know *Space Ghost* and *Samson and Goliath* had ones as well). If anyone ever finds copies of those two coloring books, please let me know!

This was the part of "The Moby Dick and Mighty Mightor show". There was one episode aired between two episodes of Mightor, it was a good if highly unusual pairing. I would really have enjoyed being in the staff meeting to hear just how this particular concept came up. "Let's have a super whale!" "Great idea! And then we can have a super caveman as well!" "It's a natural!" Thank goodness the show is played completely straight, as it wouldn't be these days.

Starring the voices of: Voices: Barry Balkin, Bobby Resnick, Don Messick, John Stephenson, Paul Stewart, Bob Diamond and Patsy Garrett.

Our Heroes:

Moby Dick- a giant, super intelligent white whale. Can speak to some sea life, and appears to have no bones on occasion. Moby uses the "giant spin" several times to defeats his various foes. The smartest creature in whatever ocean they happen to be in, he also serves as a conveyance vehicle and safety shelter for the rest of the gang.

Tom and Tubb- the boys, given to yelling "on the double bubble" and "Geronimoby!" at any given time in an episode. Tom is presented as being the slightly smarter one, while Tubb is of course, kind of tubby, and the "funnier" one and usually the less brave of the boys. Both kids are very resourceful and help Moby with his fighting strategies a lot.

Scooby- is a very smart sea lion. Usually called a seal, the presence of ears tells us what species he really is. He's usually shown to be smarter than boys in any given episode.

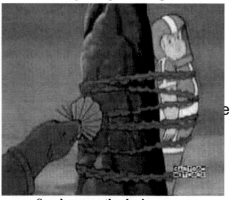

Scooby saves the day!

The Episodes:

The Sand Creatures- a strange creature is making powerful giant monsters. When the gang shows up he sends them out to attack. *The villain is never named in this one. The creatures are nicely designed.*

The Vortex Trap- Moby and the gang battle Vortan and his robotic minions to stop his invasion of Earth. *Vortan only has one henchman, but several dozen weapons. The aliens defeat themselves, more or less.*

Toadus, Ruler of the Dead Ships- our heroes wander into the Sea of Dead Ships. Toadus believes they are after his treasure and attacks them. *No giant creature for Moby to fight in this episode.*

The Shark Men- Tom and Tub are captured by Shark Men. Moby and Scooby eventually rescue them. *Tom and Tub do most of the work this time.*

The Saucer Shells- are after dolphins and the gang stops them. *Tom and Tub know the Saucer Shells already. We never see the occupants of the shells.*

The Iguana Men- Iguanus captures Tom and Tub so he can transfer their ability to breath air into his sea terrors. He will then invade the upper regions! *The Sea Terrors are mutated squid.*

The Cereb Men-the evil Cereb Men kidnap Prince Sor and want total surrender from King Trez. The gang sets off to rescue him. *Tom and Tub know the water people. The Cereb Men have cool tripod ships.*

The Iceberg Monster- a huge monsters is freed from it's icy prison. Moby battles it tooth and nail! *An action packed episode- aside from the monster, we also get a giant squid to menace Tom and Tub as well.*

The Electrifying Shocktopus- while investigating an old wreck, Tom and Tub find a treasure map. Captain Squid takes it, and then using his Shocktopus has to battle Moby. *The Shocktopus is very sleek. Scooby is the one that frees Moby.*

The Shimmering Screen- a strange shimmering portal leads our heroes to the world of the Mantanites. Our heroes go through to save a mermaid. *Tom tells Tub there's no such things as mermaids at first.*

The Sea Ark- Zortak attempts to add a sea pony to their space zoo. Moby stops them. *Nice villains, but never named as a race- we don't know if they are aliens or what.*

Soodak the Invader- Soodak attempts to invade, but Moby stops him. *Soodak's scout ships have Roman numerals on them.*

The Sinister Sea Saucer- Tom and Tub go check out a landing space capsule. They immediately assume an evil force is guiding it to the uncharted seas. Manta Menace is indeed responsible for doing that. *They go overboard on the whole "evil" motif here. Manta Menace gets away, promising revenge.*

the awesome Aquabats!

The Crab Creatures- while investigating another sunken wreck, crab people attack Tom and Tub. Tub gets captured. Moby to the rescue. *No reason is given for the Crab Creatures attack. Moby calls sawfish to help him escape.*

The Aqua-Bats- a horde of aqua-bats attack our heroes. They take Tom and Tub, but are attacked by a giant Portuguese Man-o-War. *The Man-o-war is a great looking beast. And who knew one of the most awesome bands of all time would use this name?*

T he Sea Monster- A giant fearsome fish accidentally swallows Tub. This leads to a fearsome battle between the monster and Moby. *The fish looks a bit like Dunkleosteus terrelli.*

Dunkleosteus terrelli

Moraya, the Eel Queen- Moby has a battle with "Octo". Viewing this, Moraya uses Moby to challenge her fighters. *I wonder if this octopus is well known to the boys, since they have named it. Moraya's warrior fish bears a strong resemblance to "the Iceberg Monster". The monsters do look fierce.*

The Undersea World- an seaquake opens a whole into an underwater world full of weird and strange monsters. Our heroes have to battle their way out. *An interesting idea, but needed more monsters.*

Our heroes also made an appearance in the second season of Space Ghost, helping Jan, Jace and Blip escape on of the Council of Doom's diabolical traps. Of course in the world of 1960s kid cartoons things were never wrapped up. The adventures just keep continuing to happen, and Tom and Tub never make it "home". Heck, the viewers are left with the impression the kids never were that concerned about it!

There has been no DVD release of the cartoon, but there was a VHS collection released in the 80s. Perhaps with the "burn on demand" becoming more popular a set of the series will show up.

Thunderfoot Theater presents...

From Lee to Li, an appreciation

by Chad McAlpin

Over the years I have become quite the Jet Li fan. A staple of early Cable TV was Kung Fu Theater. I would sit there mesmerized by the mystical Kung Fu prowess of the protagonists and it colored my tastes in the 80s. If it was any type of martial arts flick I would watch it. Once I discovered Bruce Lee I had found the most awesome thing. To a 9 year old me, my discovery was more significant than any discovery made by Columbus, Curie, Edison, Franklin, Pasteur or the like. I wanted to train so badly but my folks felt that with my temperament it was a bad idea. That seemed to be the beginning of the demise of my fervent love affair with Martial Arts films. Like most people, growing up meant I moved away from things I once held dear. I still loved Martial Arts films, but my dedication to watching nothing but had waned.

When I got married in '98 there was a block buster right down the road from our Apartment. One of the things we did in those early days was to go rent movies. I saw a film called Black Mask and it appealed to me. Not only did it have the trappings of being a Martial Arts film, but it also had a super hero vibe to it as comic were another of my childhood loves. I got it and enjoyed it. The action sequences were good and it had n old pulp book feel to it. I had never heard of Jet Li, and while I enjoyed that film immensely my love affair with his films had yet to take hold.

My wife had went to the aforementioned Blockbuster and remembered I had enjoyed **Black Mask** (released 1996 in Hong Kong and 1999 in the US). She remembered Jet Li's name, so she looked for another film of his for me to peruse. She found **Fist of Legend** (1994). When I put the film in it was one of those moments that you remember always. I was instantly taken back to the days of sitting mesmerized at the exploits of all my heroes on Kung Fu Theater. My love affair with martial arts films had been rekindled by watching this film. It is funny how discovering something new can instantly take you back to long distant point in time, but this film did that.

Fist of Legend was not a frame for frame remake of Bruce Lee's **Fist of Fury** (1972), but it was certainly a retelling of sorts. The story was well done and the action sequences were

 phenomenal. In my mind it had all the things I had loved as a child but was done in less cheesy manner. The dubbing better matched the movement of the actor's mouths, the sound effects didn't sound like a wet towel being flung through the air, and the overall presentation looked much nicer.

After that I hunted down any and all things Jet Li. I would do my best to convert my family and friends into becoming fans of his. Now the merits of Wushu as an actual fighting discipline can be debated, the fact he was a champion practitioner gave him more credibility in my eyes than say Jackie Chan or Sammo Hung. It seemed as if I had finally found the man to finally take the mantle of great martial arts star from the late Bruce Lee.

It has been a little over 12 years since my discovery. I own all of his films. The main things that has changed since then is the fact my collection is now on DVD as opposed to VHS. I know some deride Jet for the fact some of his films epitomized the wire fu era that was reviled, but I didn't mind them. Some of the greatest Kung Fu classics relied on fanciful fighting and this was no different in my eyes.

The simple fact of the matter is some of his films have been classics and some not so much. His foray into American Films has led to some great films but many that didn't know what to do with him. To me, it is immaterial. He resides just under Bruce in my pantheon of favorite Martial Arts stars. I love all of his films, even the "bad" ones. While I feel he has ceded his crown of top action star to Tony Jaa, I will forever hold a certain place for him and his films. Through him and his films I have found other stars that have captured my imagination. Even though Kung Fu Theater went off the air over 25 years ago, it still lives on today.

THe VaLLey OF GWaNgi
(1969)

The poster for this movie is just awesome. I can't imagine being a kid and not having to see this movie after viewing this most awesome poster. I just had the coloring book and it made me want to see the movie in the worst way ever. I had to wait til 1974 or so before it aired on late night TV, which was a big deal back then to stay up late to watch a most anticipated airing like this!

I was not disappointed at all- loads of dinosaurs and cowboys plus a beautiful woman all in one movie. It's nearly perfect! Well, maybe not, but it's a heckuva lot of fun. Also present is a grand musical score by Jerome Moross (*Wagon Train, The Warlord, The Adventures of Huckleberry Finn*), which manages to capture both a western movie and a monster movie feel quite well.

I was completely prepped for the movie, due to having the coloring book for several years before I saw the movie. So I

Gwangi makes a meal of an ornithomimus

was well aware of just when the various prehistoric critters would be making their appearances. Though I am pretty sure that I had no idea what their colors would be, so I got to use my imagination for all of that.

Fortunately Gwangi himself rather resembles a chameleon in that he changes color a few times himself in the movie. This really has no impact on the entertainment quality of the movie, but it's kind of fun to watch for now.

One of the unique things about the movie is the interesting role reversal that goes on between Tuck and TJ after Gwangi has been captured. Presumably Tuck has realized that a life chasing money isn't that satisfying and wants to settle down with TJ. It's also easy to see that TJ, seeing a chance for the "big time" now with a live dinosaur to exhibit, wants to go for a chance at success. It's understandable that after toiling for years and making no money she would want to do that, but I wonder what happened to her after the movie ended.

Gwangi also features some of Harryhausen's most dynamic animation. Nearly all of the stop-motion sequences are spectacular, except for maybe the fight with the styracosaurus. For some reason that dinosaur doesn't seem to be very visually exciting and sadly it shows against the awesome Gwangi.

Another interesting item to note is Gwangi gets a name. Most of Harryhausen's non-mythic movies feature giant animals of some form or another, which don't always lead themselves to much characterization. Gwangi is mean and out for a meal always. He kills the poor little ornithomimus and then drops it as soon as he sees the cowboys. Now that's a beast out for blood!

Gwangi is also an excellent design. One sees right away he's the master of his valley and nothing can stand in his way.

THE VALLEY OF GWANGI has been released on DVD in a fine looking presentation. The picture looks great, there's a nice extra or two, plus the trailer. It's too bad that whoever is in charge of the DVD covers chose a misleading if interesting Italian poster to base it on, despite Mr. Harryhausen's personal pleading for them to use the original poster. The cover is not a good fit for the movie, and doesn't do anything to encourage a person to buy the DVD. I'm starting to think there's some VP exec named "William H. Gwange" at Warner Brothers who wants this movie to fail every time it's released in any form at all.

Another tie in released was this comic book. It has the awesome poster adapted into a great cover, but the interior art, but Jack Sparling, looks incredibly rushed. It's highly likely all Jack had to go on is black and white stills, as "TJ" is a brunette throughout the book, and none of the dinosaurs looks a thing like they do in the movie. There could be a whole article about the various quality of Dell-Gold Key comics, but I'll let someone else far more informed about such matters write it. Or at least tell us where to read it.

Case in point- this is a pretty dynamic drawing of the cowboys meeting Gwangi for the first time. Nothing like it ever happened in the movie, nor does the struthiomimus look like the drawing. Had I gotten the comic book as a kid, I would have enjoyed it. Seeing it now with more discerning eyes I have to wonder why Harryhausen's films have never had many good comic book adaptions. Marvel Comics published three issues based on the first two Harryhausen Sinbad movies, which are the best looking versions out there.

GWANGI may be my second favorite Harryhausen movie, right after ONE MILLION YEARS, BC. No surprise to me they both feature dinosaurs.

El Baron Brakola

Jeff Goodhartz

Awfully sporting of Video Search of Miami to subtitle what has up until now, been one of the tougher Santo pictures to track down. It was worth the wait as this turned out to be one of the better of the fifty or so features from the Man in the Silver Mask. It was the last of four consecutive films he appeared in from producer Luis Enrique Vergara (following "*The Witches Attack*", The *Diabolical Hatchet*" and "*Grave Robbers*") and may be the best of this bunch. Vergara's group was on the eccentric side, even for a Lucha Libre film and had noticeably smaller budgets than others of this vintage. But what they lacked money-wise, they made up for with a higher level of action and energy. This is easily one of the more action packed Santo films I've seen.

This is another of the "Colonial Era" Santos that features a prolonged flashback showing how Santo's ancestor created enemy that would come back haunt our hero in modern times. That enemy is the evil. selfish, self centered son of a bitch known as Baron Brakola (sounds a lot like Dra... oh, never mind). Brak is portrayed Fernando Oses, who is arguably Santo's best screen adversary. He is a truly brutish, threatening presence and their numerous battles throughout are far more brutal and realistic than the usual fare to found in these films. The two protagonists seem to know each other's moves well (likely from much actual ring experience) and go at it with

la pelicula!

fairly reckless abandon, leading to mucho excitement.

One unintentionally comical moment occurs when Brak is fended off (in the ring) by a crucifix. Now throughout the film, Brak has been nothing less than imposing. Somebody must have told Oses to really play up this moment because he basically screams and flails his hands like a woman before fleeing the ring. After I stopped laughing (and laughing) I suddenly questioned why he didn't bother turning into a bat (which he had done earlier in the film)? Oh well, this is entry in the series is lots of fun for both the right and wrong reasons.

4 Stars (out of a possible 5)

Maki's 13 Steps

Jeff Goodhartz

The film opens on a particularly grim scene. Two young women are tied to railroad tracks, topless and spread eagle. Into the frame appears an all female gang, obviously the ones responsible for the girls' predicament. As they torture and beat the two unfortunates (and threaten to do worse), the scene grows even grimmer. Suddenly, the "festivities" are interrupted by an approaching lone figure, dressed in a  long white overcoat. It is Etsuko Shihomi. The music swells as she (in an amazing low angle shot) throws off the coat to reveal a black uniform, complete with red gloves... and the number 13 prominently displayed on her shirt. As the credits roll, she single handedly lays waste to the entire girl gang AND the accompanying male gang that arrive on the scene , ready to attack our (super) heroine. Punches, kicks, flips and a gory eye gouging (for good measure) are all on display as the freeze framed credits continue to roll. Over the carnage, a superhero ballad plays, sung by Shihomi herself. Could this be the greatest opening sequence in the history of action cinema?

Amazingly, it only picks up from there. The term "action packed" has been overused ad nauseum, but it applies here in spades. There is barely a slow second in this economic 78 minute action classic and it never once gets tedious to watch. The action builds properly and exhilaratingly, thanks to the sure hand of director Naito Makoto. I'm unfamiliar with Makoto's work and he appears to have directed only sporadically over the last several decades. But if this film (full title; Maki's 13 Steps; Young Nobility) is any indication, he should've been give many, many more opportunities.

Then there is Maki herself, portrayed by the incomparable Etsuko "Sue" Shihomi. Shihomi is without question, my all time favorite fighting femme and this is her masterpiece. As Shinichi "Sonny" Chiba's top student, she combines the cute girl next door looks with an absolute ferociousness to her performances that is quite alarming, even to those already familiar with her work. So strong and so thorough is Shihomi here that by the climax where she alone confronts a gang of fifty or so Yakuza with the line, "Maki and her 13 steps will send you all to hell!" you fully and unhesitatingly believe that she can and will do just that. The story basically shows the running battle between Maki and her girl gang as they butt heads with a powerful Yakuza gang. Along the way, Maki incurs the vengeance of a spoiled gang daughter she had previously humiliated and confronts her equal, an ex boxer who turns out to be an honorable fighter. Both characters go from foe to tenuous ally as the Yakuza head alternately dishonors both. This makes for a great, twisty tale to go along with the almost constant karate confrontations.

Maki's 13 Steps (even with subtitles I am not certain what the 13 Steps is all about, but never mind) comes with my highest recommendation. Where for art thou, Etsuko Shihomi?

Gigantis, the Fire Monster (1959)

What do you do when you have a smash hit of a movie? Make a quick sequel of course. The second Godzilla film was released in Japan less than a year after the first one.

And since *Godzilla, King of the Monsters!* was a huge hit over here as well, you'd think it would be a no-brainer that the sequel would be brought over right away.

Surprise! It took about four years, and what we got was not quite the same movie Toho made. Add to that a convoluted story called "*The Volcano Monsters*" and one wonders how it ever got released here at all! I really like the title "The Volcano Monsters" but am kind of glad they didn't cut this movie up even more to make it.

Once I had realized there was a "series" of Godzilla movies, I started keeping track of the ones I had seen. This was the one movie that never aired in CO as long as I had been scouring the TV Guide for creature features. It wasn't until about 1984 or so, after cable came to town that it aired on a Godzilla Marathon on the USA Network, I believe, that I got to see it.

original title card

Oddly enough, it was one of the first Godzilla movies available commercially from GoodTimes, back in the late 80s, under the "Gigantis" title, at first. It was later replaced with the now Toho-mandated "Godzilla Raids Again" title, which was video generated (the new DVD presentation also has this title). There used to be a rumor that there was a different version of the movie out in the world, but it has never surfaced since I've been a fan.

Back in the old days, before home video, before wikipedia and pre-internets, there was a lot of speculation about this movie. Many people assumed it was exactly the same as the Japanese version, since there were no US actors inserted into it like *Godzilla, King of the Monsters!* had done. I can't in good conscience call Godzilla "Gigantis" though. I'll be using his real name throughout this article.

There were however, some interesting and rather inexplicable shots of dinosaurs added into the movie. No one knows why the King Brothers decided to add this stock footage to this movie, as the effects are decidedly far beneath what Tsuburaya was showing us already. I remember reading in several articles for various magazines that the stop-motion in this movie was so bad it's no wonder Tsuburaya decided to abandon it for the rest of his career (he used the technique sporadically, anyway).

The origin of these shots is also a bit of a mystery. Some of the footage of "dinosaurs" obviously came from the 1948 potboiler *Unknown Island* (worthy of a review in a future issue as well) but where the aforementioned stop-motion came from is still, well, unknown. Some have claimed it was from a Mexican movie and some have claimed it was from science films. The world may never know.

This was the first movie to show two giant monsters fighting to the death in a modern day city. Godzilla and Angilas wipe out a large cityscape in their battle to the death. These are some great scenes, made very surreal by the change of camera speeds. The monsters fight more like animals than what we would get used to later on in the series.

It's not the best Godzilla sequel out there, but it's not the worst. Despite what some fans have said, the US version isn't any better or any worse than it's Japanese counterpart.

Contributors page:

- **Tara DeVeau**- All she ever wanted was to live at the beach, paint with the sunrise and read till the sunset... but Life is what happens while you are making other plans...

- **Christopher Elam**- see his bio in the Owari section!

- **Jeff Goodhartz**- Wanders the land in search of enlightenment, but does so within the confines of his New Jersey apartment. Spends most of his waking hours watching funky movies from the Far (and occasionally Middle) East

- **Chad McAlpin**- Could have been a Doctor had he filled his brain with usual knowledge instead of being able to tell you everything about Star Wars, Pro Wrestling, Jet Li flicks, Transformers, and Comic Books.

- **Dan Ross**- was a fan of Tokusatsu long before he knew what Tokusatsu was. He is a full time animator and occasional illustrator who still enjoys giant monsters and super robots any chance he can get.

- **Mike Lawyer**- Born in 1971, Mike has been a die hard monster fan since the age of 4 and an afternoon TV showing of King Kong vs Godzilla! Many drive-in monster movies and 2 great UHF channels in the late 70s and throughout the 80s provided a steady stream of monsters from the classic Universals, Hammer,AIP, kaiju and even Paul Naschy. Mike has been married for almost 19 years and has two teenage sons who also appreciate the classics. Mike lives with his family and his collection of monster toys, kits, posters and DVDs in beautiful upstate NY at the foothills of the Adirondack mountains where he is always hoping to spot sasquatch.

OUTtakes:

I hope that the next issue of Xenorama doesn't take ten years, or even two years to publish. It should be easier these days, but it seems like life moves faster and faster every year.

I seem to have fallen into the trap of having so much great material that I put it all into this zine at once, resulting in a 100 page monster. Well, OK, 60 page monster. I took a few of my articles out, saving them for the next zine. Now that I've found a reliable self publishing process I'm pretty sure it won't take so long. Late into writing this I found out that I could print in color. How cool is that?

Here's the part of the magazine I used to sign by hand, but since it's all computerized now, I'll just say thanks for reading and stay tuned for the next issue...
-David

The first version of the awesome cover.

39963831R00025

Made in the USA
Middletown, DE
30 January 2017